BiG QUESTiONS About the UNIVERSE

ALEX FRITH & ALICE JAMES

Illustrated by **DAVID J PLANT**

Designed by **ZOE WRAY & TABITHA BLORE**

Universe expert: **DR. ED BLOOMER, ROYAL OBSERVATORY GREENWICH**

I'll be answering all these questions. Well, the ones scientists HAVE answers for, at least...

How high do astronauts fly?

How much does it cost to go to space?

How many galaxies are there?

What's a black hole?

Why is space stuff round?

Do stars ever stop shining?

What's the weirdest object in space?

Will people ever live on Mars?

How many moons are there?

How does the Sun work?

How do you become an astronaut?

Does the universe have an edge?

Usborne Quicklinks

For links to websites where you can find answers to more questions about the universe, visit an astronaut on the ISS and follow a robot rover on Mars – right NOW – go to **usborne.com/Quicklinks** and type in the title of this book. Please follow the internet safety guidelines at Usborne Quicklinks. Children should be supervised online.

Contents

What exactly IS the universe?

The universe is EVERYTHING – it's you and me, it's the planet we live on, it's the Sun, and it's all of the space in between and all around – and beyond.

Is the UNIVERSE the same thing as SPACE?

Almost. Most of the universe is space, but it also includes places such as our planet, Earth, which *aren't* space.

I have lots more questions...

Excellent – we have lots of answers for you. And don't worry, no question is too big or too small.

CHAPTER 1

The basics

Where is space?

Space is up beyond the sky.
The part of sky you can see in the daytime is called the **atmosphere**. It doesn't have a solid edge, it gets thinner and thinner and fades away to become...

space.

So, space is up there?

But what's in it? Where does it start? How far does it go?

It's not entirely possible to answer any of those questions, but let's give it a try...

What's space made of?

Space isn't *made of* anything. It's literally the opposite of *anything*. Space is an emptiness. It's the word we use to describe the place where there is nothing. Scientists sometimes call it a **vacuum**.

So is space completely empty, then?

Well, actually, no. The space between big things such as stars and planets does contain *some* things: comets, asteroids, pieces of dust, wisps of gas. If you counted all that up, there would be rather a lot of stuff in space. But space is SO BIG, it is *mostly* empty. And most of the stuff in space is incredibly small, sometimes as small as a single **atom**.

> What's an atom, please?

> Atoms are the pieces that stuff is made from. *Incredibly tiny* pieces – so small that there are literally millions of them on the head of a pin.

Imagine a box just big enough to fit a person inside.

If that box contained a section of space, it might only contain between 1 and 10 *atoms*.

And that's all.

Where does space begin?

People don't agree. Earth is surrounded by an atmosphere, which is made of air. Air is made up of single atoms, as well as atoms joined together in clumps called molecules. Close to Earth, there are LOTS of atoms and molecules, and the air is very THICK. Further away, there are fewer and the air is very THIN. It's up to individual people to decide how thin the air has to be to count as space.

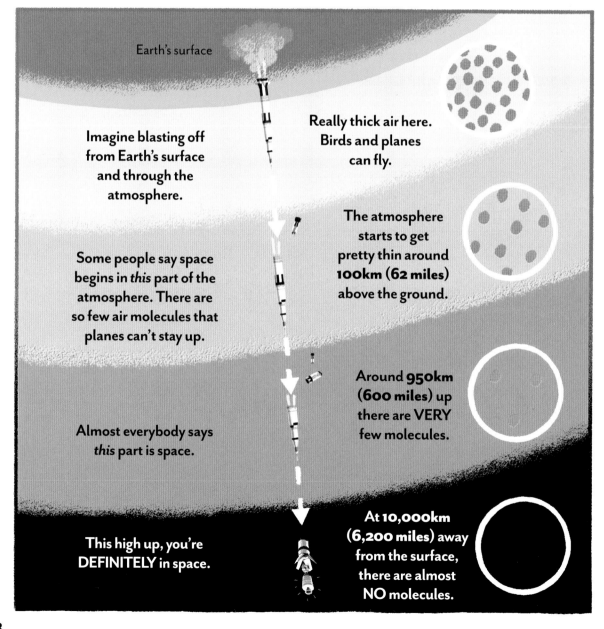

Earth's surface

Imagine blasting off from Earth's surface and through the atmosphere.

Really thick air here. Birds and planes can fly.

Some people say space begins in *this* part of the atmosphere. There are so few air molecules that planes can't stay up.

The atmosphere starts to get pretty thin around **100km (62 miles)** above the ground.

Around **950km (600 miles)** up there are VERY few molecules.

Almost everybody says *this* part is space.

This high up, you're DEFINITELY in space.

At **10,000km (6,200 miles)** away from the surface, there are almost NO molecules.

How high do astronauts fly?

Over 100km (62 miles) high. Anyone who has flown this high, or higher, has earned the right to call themselves an astronaut, according to most space agencies. This height is often known as the **Kármán Line** (named after the person who first defined it), and it's very interesting to scientists. Here's why.

Whoosh!

Imagine you're a rock...
...hurtling towards Earth.

Many thousands of miles above the surface, you might fly past a space telescope or some satellites.

You'd pass the International Space Station around 400km (250 miles) from Earth's surface.

MUCH lower down, you'd hit the Kármán Line, and you'd find yourself pushing really hard on the air molecules in front of you. This creates something called **ram pressure**, and it makes rocks BURN.

The exact height of the line varies a little at different times and in different parts of the world.

Kármán Line ↗

Most space rocks burn up entirely while still in the sky.

This is a photo showing a rock burning up as it hits the Kármán Line. Scientists call it a **meteor** – most people call it a shooting star.

Ground

How BIG is the universe?

Unknown. *Completely* unknown. But here's *part* of an answer:
if you were flying through space at the speed of light – which is the fastest
possible speed that exists – you would never, *ever* come to an end.
Whichever direction you fly in, you'd only ever find MORE space.
So, in a sense, the universe goes on *forever*.

Does the universe have an edge?

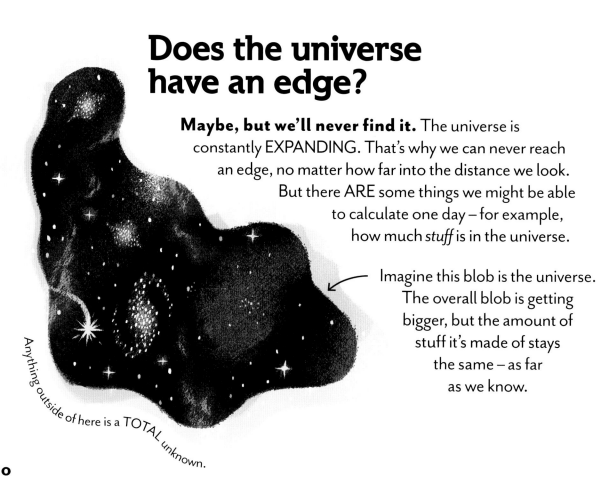

Maybe, but we'll never find it. The universe is
constantly EXPANDING. That's why we can never reach
an edge, no matter how far into the distance we look.
But there ARE some things we might be able
to calculate one day – for example,
how much *stuff* is in the universe.

Imagine this blob is the universe.
The overall blob is getting
bigger, but the amount of
stuff it's made of stays
the same – as far
as we know.

Anything outside of here is a TOTAL unknown.

How far is the furthest star?

More than 28 billion light years away.
At least, that's as far as we've *seen*. But there are definitely more stars *even further* away; their light just hasn't reached Earth yet.

What are light years?

Light years are a way to describe really, REALLY long distances.
1 light year is the distance that a beam of light travels in a year.
That's around 10 trillion km (or 6 trillion miles). So something that's
28 billion light years away is…

…seriously far away.

Imagine that you'd heard about a new star that had just been born (technically this is impossible – but you can still *imagine* it), but it was 10 light years away. You'd have to wait…

…and wait…

…for ten years…

…until its light reached Earth.

Did you know, looking into space also means *looking back in time*? When you DO see that star, you're seeing it as it was 10 years ago.

What does space look like through a telescope?

It depends on the telescope. Normal telescopes, sometimes called **optical telescopes**, magnify what you see through them, making far away things look bigger and easier to see. But there are other types of telescope that can detect things that human eyes can't see at all.

How can a telescope see something I can't?

It's to do with the way that light travels. It moves in *waves*, and human eyes can only see *certain shapes* of light waves.

Light waves travel in repeating patterns, which come in different lengths. These can be short, long, or anywhere in between.

Here's a diagram of a light pattern with a short wavelength:

Here's one with a long wavelength:

These squashed up and stretched out wavelengths are invisible to humans. But people have built machines that can and do detect them.

What do normal telescopes see?

Optical telescopes can see the same wavelengths of light as human eyes – medium-sized ones. These are what make up the rainbow, and together they're known as **visible light**.

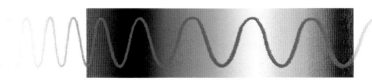

Violet is the shortest...   **...and red is the longest.**

What other telescopes are there?

People have built telescopes to detect all the different waves: gamma rays, X-rays, infrared, ultraviolet, microwaves and radio waves. Using computers to convert these wavelengths into images we can see, these telescopes make invisible things visible. By using more than one kind of telescope, astronomers can build up spectacular pictures of things in space – but they're not what you could see with your own eyes.

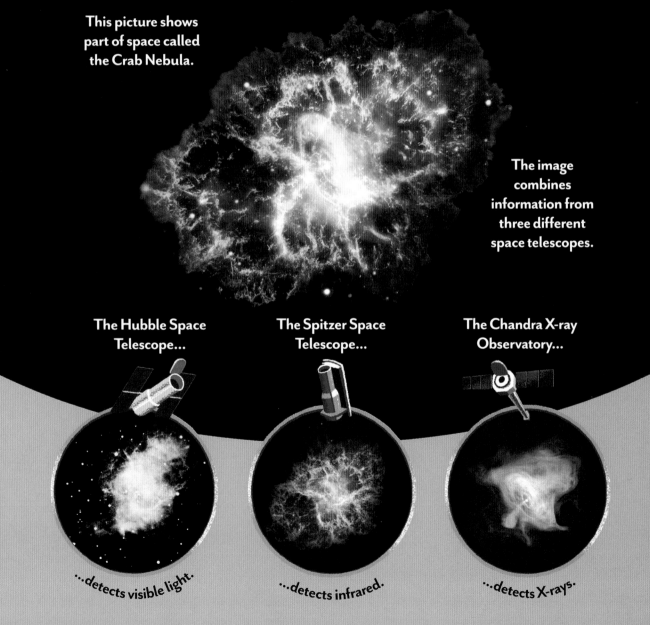

This picture shows part of space called the Crab Nebula.

The image combines information from three different space telescopes.

The Hubble Space Telescope...

The Spitzer Space Telescope...

The Chandra X-ray Observatory...

...detects visible light.

...detects infrared.

...detects X-rays.

Why are so many things in space ROUND?

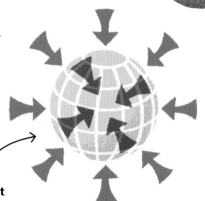

Because of gravity. Gravity is a pulling force. It pulls stuff together, and works in every direction. The simplest shape that is equal in every direction is a round ball – more properly called a **sphere**.

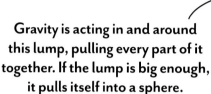

Gravity is acting in and around this lump, pulling every part of it together. If the lump is big enough, it pulls itself into a sphere.

Are planets *perfectly* round?

No. For example, Earth *looks* round, but it's not a perfect sphere. Around the middle, called the **equator**, it bulges a little.

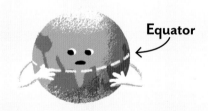

EARTH

Equator

Do other planets have a bulge at their equators?

Yes, almost all of them do. Saturn has the BIGGEST bulge.

SATURN

What isn't round?

Plenty of things, as long as they are small enough.
For instance, Mars has two small moons, called Deimos and Phobos. They're lumpy and irregular, and made of tough rocks similar to rocks you might find at a beach.

MARS ➚

So why *aren't* small space things round?

Deimos

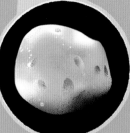

On average about 12km (7.5 miles) across

Phobos

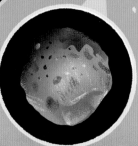

Roughly 22km (13.7 miles) across

Well, Deimos is so small that its gravity isn't strong enough to pull it into a sphere.

Phobos is bigger, but it isn't actually a single rock. It's lots of pieces of rock – a lumpy pile of rubble with a thin outer crust.

Some small objects in space are potato-shaped. Look at these rocks. The biggest is FAR bigger than Phobos and Deimos – but it's still so small that its gravity can't pull it into a neat sphere.

951 Gaspra

12km (7.5 miles)

433 Eros

17km (10.5 miles)

243 Ida

31.5km (19.5 miles)

4 Vesta

525km (326 miles)

How did the universe begin?

In the beginning, there was nothing. Then, there was...

THE BIG BANG!

Actually, that's not QUITE true...

For a start, there wasn't any kind of *bang,* big or small. This is just the name scientists use to describe the events that did happen. It wasn't noisy at all.

That's because sound only exists when there's stuff for sound to travel through – such as air or water.

As far as anybody knows, what *really* happened was that the universe just suddenly appeared. And in that moment, time began, as well as space.

What was it like?

Imagine this blob contains the ENTIRE UNIVERSE.

Everything within the blob is squashed up and SUPER hot.

In the instant after it appeared, that blob INFLATED.

Ever since then, it has been gradually expanding and cooling.

What does the universe look like?

It's not possible to say. And it's incredibly difficult to draw – because the universe is made up of *time* as well as *space*. When people try to depict it they have to show how it has *changed over time*.

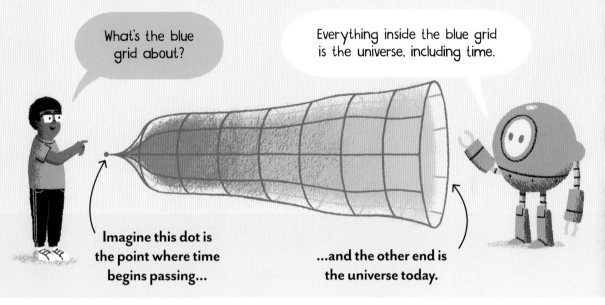

What's the blue grid about?

Everything inside the blue grid is the universe, including time.

Imagine this dot is the point where time begins passing...

...and the other end is the universe today.

What was it like at first?

Really, utterly, brain-meltingly HOT. For hundreds of thousands of years, the entire universe was so hot that the very things that stuff itself is made of, atoms, *could not exist*. Even the parts that make up atoms, known as **subatomic particles**, could barely hold together.

For around 370,000 years, there were only **subatomic particles.**

Eventually, things cooled down enough that they could clump together to make the first **atoms**...

...and some years after that, these atoms joined together to make the first **stars.**

Shall we join up?

Not yet.

Now's good.

I'm going to be a star!

CHAPTER 2

The solar system

What does "solar" mean?

It means to do with the Sun. So, the "solar system" means the collection of things that orbit the Sun. Other stars have their own systems, too. We know a little about OUR system – especially about the big objects that are close to the Sun. But the solar system is VAST, and the outer reaches beyond Pluto hold many mysteries.

THE SUN
(a star)

MERCURY
(one of eight planets)

VENUS

EARTH

THE MOON
(a moon)

MARS

What's...
...the Sun?

It's a STAR – that is, it's a giant ball, made of super-hot stuff called plasma. The solar system only has one star – but many other systems have two, known as **binary stars**.

...a planet?

An object that orbits a star. They're always round, or at least, round-ish, but in other ways, planets can be VERY different from each other.

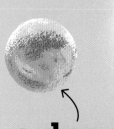

...a dwarf planet?

A roundish object that orbits a star. They're very similar to planets – but they have some differences, for example they are smaller and tend to have more objects closer to them than planets. But scientists don't all agree on what a dwarf planet is.

...a moon?

An object that orbits a planet or a dwarf planet. It can be big or small, and can have any shape. Astronomers sometimes call them **natural satellites**.

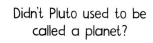

Didn't Pluto used to be called a planet?

Yes, that's right. Ceres, another dwarf planet, was considered a planet, too, 200 years ago. The definitions of what's in each group sometimes changes.

What are planets made from?

We don't know *in detail*. Even the Earth's core holds some mysteries. But some planets are made from rocks and metal; others are mostly gas. The only rocky planets in the solar system are Mercury, Venus, Earth and Mars. As far as we know, all planets are made up in layers...

Inside EARTH (a rocky planet)

- Gas
- Solid rock
- Semi-solid rock
- Liquid metal
- Solid metal

The solar system also has four planets known as **gas giants**: Jupiter, Saturn, Uranus and Neptune. These planets are BIG, and might be made of liquid as well as gas.

Inside JUPITER (a gas giant)

- Thin gas
- Thick gas
- Metal that might be liquid

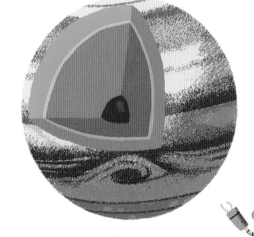

Can you land a spaceship on Jupiter?

HIGHLY doubtful. The outer layers of gas are probably too thick to fly into, and even if you could, scientists don't think there's a solid core to land on anyway.

21

What's an orbit?

The path that an object takes as it moves through space around a bigger object.

In our solar system, planets, asteroids and comets all orbit the Sun, while moons and human-made satellites orbit different planets. Each dotted line in this picture represents an orbit. Some of them are rounder than others.

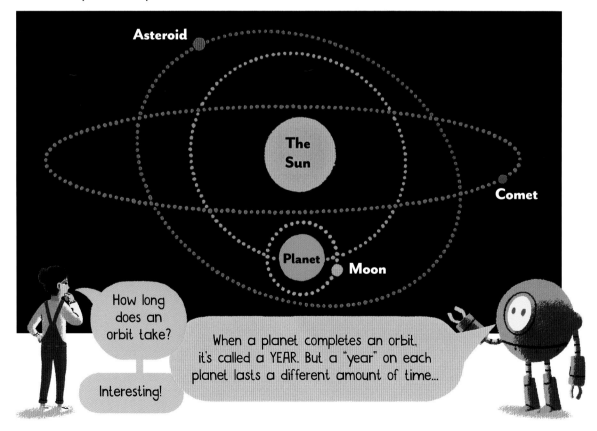

How long is a year on Mercury?

88 Earth days. That's less than a quarter of an Earth year – but Mercury doesn't have to travel nearly as far to orbit the Sun.

YEAR LENGTHS

Mercury year = 88 days

Venus year = 225 days

Earth year = 365 days

Mars year = 687 days

Jupiter year = 4,333 days

Saturn year = 10,759 days

Uranus year = 30,687 days

Neptune year = 60,190 days

Axis

How long is a day on Mercury?

1,408 hours. That means it's spinning around something called its **axis** VEEEEERRRRRRY SLOOOOOOWLY, compared to Earth. All planets spin around.

What actually IS a day?

A full DAY is the time it takes for a planet to spin around on its axis once.

DAY LENGTHS

Mercury day = 1,408 hours	**Jupiter** day = 10 hours
Venus day = 5,832 hours	**Saturn** day = 11 hours
Earth day = 24 hours	**Uranus** day = 17 hours
Mars day = 25 hours	**Neptune** day = 16 hours

What's an asteroid?

A space rock that orbits the Sun. Asteroids are smaller than planets and dwarf planets, and come in all sorts of shapes.

How often do asteroids hit planets?

No one knows – but it's at least a few times every single day.

Sometimes, an asteroid's orbit takes it too close to a planet, and it gets pulled down onto that planet. Then it breaks up into smaller rocks called *meteorites*.

How many asteroids are there?

Over 1 million – and that's only counting the ones that are larger than 1km (3,280ft) wide. There are definitely more.

There's a part of the solar system between Mars and Jupiter that is home to loads of asteroids. It's known as the ASTEROID BELT – but this name can be misleading...

...because there are on average many thousands of miles of empty space between the asteroids. It's *not* a thick field full of asteroids.

Do asteroids have names?

Yes. But they have a number, too, which comes first.

1 Ceres is so big, it's classified as a dwarf planet. Scientists still call it an asteroid, too, because it's in the asteroid belt.

2 Pallas

Here are the first seven asteroids to be discovered and named. New asteroids are discovered almost every day.

3 Juno

4 Vesta

5 Astraea

6 Hebe

7 Iris

What's a comet?

An icy object with an eccentric orbit. Comets move around their star in stretched-out orbits described as **eccentric**. They pass very close to the star at some points, but at other times can be EXTREMELY far away.

The Sun

Comet

Earth

As a comet passes close to the Sun, some of its icy body BOILS OFF into space, leaving a trail that people can see from Earth.

Do comets have names?

Yes. Most comets have at least two names. One is given for the year it was first spotted, and another is often given for the person or machine that found it.

So far, astronomers have found over 4,500 comets – but there may be ONE TRILLION in our solar system alone. Most are very far off, in a distant region known as the **Oort Cloud**. Nobody knows much about this part of space.

Is that a comet?

Yes, that's a photo of C/1995 O1, the first new comet observed in the year 1995. It's also known as *Comet Hale-Bopp*, named after two people who discovered it at the same time as each other.

How many moons are there?

Astronomers have discovered more than 200 moons in our solar system – SO FAR. Mercury and Venus have none, Earth has one, and Mars has two. Here you can see the names of moons of the four gas giant planets, from largest to smallest. Some have other objects orbiting them that are so tiny, they're known as **moonlets**.

Neptune has **14** moons.

Triton
Proteus Nereid
Larissa Galataea Despina
Thalassa Halimede Naiad
Neso Sao Laomedeia
Psamathe Hippocamp

Uranus has **27** moons.

Titania
Oberon Umbriel
Ariel Miranda Sycorax
Puck Portia Juliet Belinda
Cressida Rosalind Caliban
Desdemona Bianca Prospero
Setebos Ophelia Cordelia
Stephano Perdita Mab
Francisco Margaret Ferdinand
Cupid Trinculo

Jupiter has at least **80** moons. Here are the largest that have official names.

Ganymede Callisto Io
Europa Amalthea Himalia Thebe
Elara Pasiphae Metis Carme Sinope Lysithea
Ananke Adrastea Leda Callirrhoe Themisto Iocaste
Praxidike Taygete Kalyke Megaclite Dia Helike Harpalyke
Hermippe Thyone Chaldene Aoede Eukelade Isonoe Eirene
Autonoe Ersa Carpo Euanthe Aitne Erinome Eurydome Hegemone
Arche Pandia Euporie Eupheme Thelxinoe Orthosie Mneme Herse Kale
Philophrosyne Kallichore Pasithee Kore Cyllene Sponde Valetudo

Most moon names come from Greek, Roman, Viking, Inuit and Celtic mythology.
Many of Uranus's moons are named after characters from plays by William Shakespeare.

Titan   Rhea   Iapetus   Dione   Tethy

Enceladus   Mimas   Hyperion   Phoebe   Janu

Epimetheus   Prometheus   Pandora   Siarnaq   Heler

Albiorix   Atlas   Pan   Telesto   Paaliaq   Calypso   Ym

Kiviuq   Tarvos   Ijiraq   Erriapus   Skathi   Hyrrokk

Daphnis   Tarqeq   Mundilfari   Narvi   Suttun

Thrymr   Bestla   Kari   Bebhionn   Skoll   Gre

Jarnsaxa   Bergelmir   Hati   Aegir   Surt

Loge   Fornjot   Pallene   Farbau

Fenrir   Methone   Polydeuc

Anthe   Aegae

Saturn has at least **83** moons ... and many, many moonlets. Only 53 have official names.

How many dwarf planets are there?

So far, astronomers have discovered five dwarf planets in our solar system, but there are probably more.

Can dwarf planets have moons?

Yes. Pluto has 5, Eris has 1, Haumea has 2 and Makemake has 1.

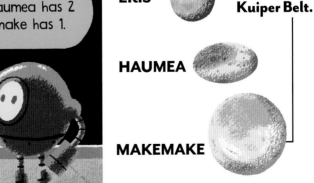

DWARF PLANETS

CERES — Found in between Mars and Jupiter.

PLUTO

ERIS — Found in a far-off region called the **Kuiper Belt.**

HAUMEA

MAKEMAKE

Why is Earth special?

Because it has water – masses and masses of liquid water.
So much water that you can see it from space. This makes Earth look different to the other planets.

In, around and on that water are MILLIONS of living things. As far as we know at the moment, that makes the Earth *unique*.

But why is there so much water on Earth?

We can't fully answer that – yet. But we know that all life on the planet depends on it.

Anything else unique about Earth?

It's the only planet we know where the land can *move*. You can't feel it, but slowly, way beneath your feet, it IS.

The Earth's crust – the part just below the land and sea – is made of moving parts called **tectonic plates**.

When the plates shift, the movement recycles and spreads out crucial nutrients that living things rely on.

Where did life come from?

Nobody really knows. We know *how* life is able to survive on Earth, but we don't know *why* it's there in the first place. The main thing that makes Earth habitable, is that it's in a patch of the solar system scientists call...

...the **GOLDILOCKS ZONE**.

Why's it called THAT??

It's because of a fairy tale about a girl with curly golden hair who wanted to eat porridge that was not too hot, not too cold...

...but just right.

On Mercury...
...it's too hot.

On Neptune...
...it's too cold.

On Earth...
...just enough sunshine reaches us.

Life would burn up in an instant from the extreme sunshine.

Life would freeze because warming heat from the Sun can't reach that far.

It's warm enough that there's liquid water, but not so warm it all evaporates. Also, Earth's atmosphere holds in the heat, and deflects dangerous radiation.

Is there life on other planets?

We don't think so, at least, not in the solar system. Some scientists say that Venus and Mars are in the Goldilocks zone *too*, which means these planets are the most likely places to show signs of life – and they do have *some* promising features.

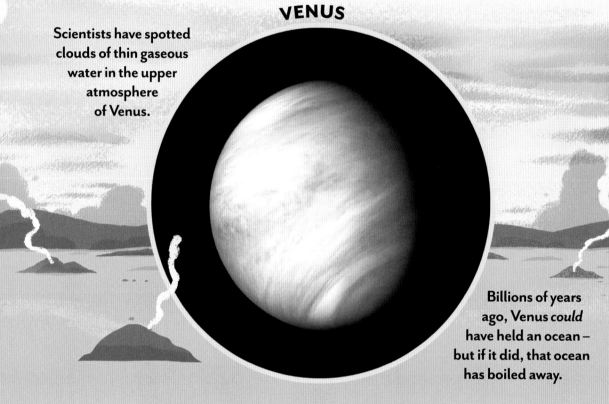

VENUS

Scientists have spotted clouds of thin gaseous water in the upper atmosphere of Venus.

Billions of years ago, Venus *could* have held an ocean – but if it did, that ocean has boiled away.

However, in 2020, scientists got a first glimpse at life-sustaining chemicals in the atmosphere of Venus.

BREAKING NEWS!! Life on Venus?

We're one step closer to finding out.

We think we've found a chemical called phosphine! On Earth, it's mainly made by living things...

It COULD be evidence that there USED TO BE life on Venus. Maybe. Perhaps. Possibly not, though. Let's not get too excited.

Rovers exploring Mars have found evidence of water. Not a giant lake or anything, but some ice, and water molecules trapped in rocks.

MARS

BLEEP BLOOP
HOOO
WATERRRRR

They've also found evidence of crucial chemicals under the surface that could hint at life.

Why is water a big deal?

Where there's water, there could be life. At least, that's what astrobiologists (space-life scientists) say. On Earth, almost nothing can survive without water — so the same might be true on other planets, too.

Where else is there water?

On several moons, and on Mercury, too. There's plenty of water, if you know where to look (and don't mind what form it comes in...). Here are just some of the places that scientists have found water, or *expect* to find it.

ENCELADUS

This moon of Saturn spews water from icy geysers. Under its ice crust scientists think the surface of this moon might be ENTIRELY ocean.

GANYMEDE

This moon of Jupiter might have a warm, wet, salty ocean under its thick crust.

EUROPA

This moon of Jupiter is covered in ice. There are lines visible on the icy surface that prove liquid water has recently been flowing around.

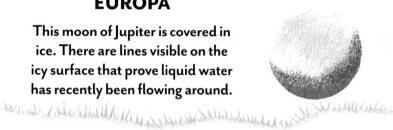

MIMAS

This moon of Saturn is basically a snowball.

CALLISTO

This moon of Jupiter has an ice crust almost 125km (78 miles) thick. That's a LOT of ice.

MERCURY

May be too hot to hold onto water, but it does hold *ice* in shaded craters at its poles.

Every discovery of new ice or water is exciting and significant – and scientists are making new discoveries all the time. What we know about where water is changes each year.

Meanwhile, on the dark side of the Moon...

Where did water on Earth come from?

Experts think there are two likely options.

1. Water, in the form of ice, came to Earth on comets. These comets crashed onto the surface and released their ice.

2. Billions of years ago, under Earth's crust, hot rocks and gases churned together, setting off of chemical reactions. These set off eruptions of steam that cooled into... water.

Option 2 is very hard to check. Astronomers *have* checked option 1, by examining the ice on a comet. It wasn't *quite* the same as ice on Earth – but they need to check lots more comets before ruling out option 1 entirely.

CHAPTER 3

Secrets of stars

How many stars are there?

More than we can count. Literally – because we can only see part of the universe. But in that part of the universe, astronomers have calculated there are somewhere between 10 sextillion and 1 septillion stars.

That sounds like a LOT. How big is 1 septillion?

A septillion is 1,000,000,000,000,000, 000,000,000 stars – more than there are grains of sand on Earth! But without a telescope you can only see a few thousand.

What ACTUALLY is a star?

A star is, usually, a giant sphere that radiates HUGE amounts of heat and light.

What do you mean, "usually"?

Well, stars exist for millions or even *billions* of years, and go through different stages across their lifetimes. And they come in different types, too.

What type of star is the Sun?

It's known as a G-Type Main Sequence star.
(And it's sometimes called a yellow dwarf, too.)

What's the Sun made of?

Mostly it's two gases – hydrogen and helium.
Except they're SO HOT, they're not in gas form.
They're in an extreme form known as **plasma**.
The Sun looks as if it's on fire – but it's not
burning; it's glowing with intense light.

Can astronauts get close to the Sun?

That is not a good idea! But in 2025, an uncrewed spacecraft called the Parker Solar Probe will get within 7 million km (4.3 million miles).

How hot is the Sun?

It's around 15 million°C (27 million°F) at its hottest part,
in the core. The coolest part of the Sun – at the surface – is still
hotter than the hottest part of Earth – the Earth's core.

How does the Sun work?

It's like a factory that turns hydrogen into helium... and light.

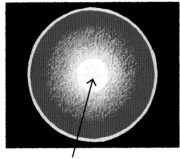

In the core, billions and **billions** of very hot hydrogen atoms are packed so tightly they collide constantly.

Lots of those atoms don't bounce off each other, though. Instead, they join together, or **fuse**.

Whenever hydrogen atoms fuse, they create hot helium atoms, and great bursts of light.

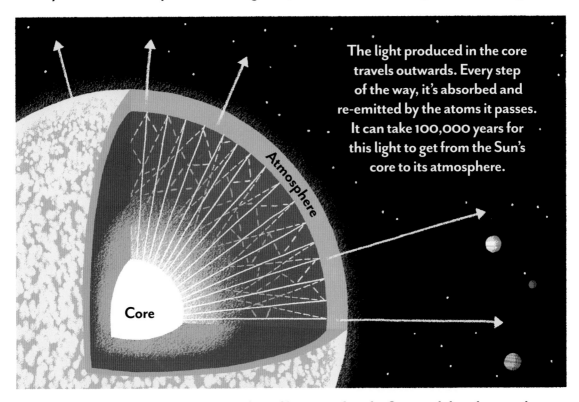

The light produced in the core travels outwards. Every step of the way, it's absorbed and re-emitted by the atoms it passes. It can take 100,000 years for this light to get from the Sun's core to its atmosphere.

Atmosphere

Core

Astronomers know there are a number of layers within the Sun, and that the way they interact is complicated. One of the few things they know for sure is that light from the atmosphere beams out into space, and eventually reaches the planets.

What other types of stars are there?

Lots and *lots.* If you're talking about Main Sequence stars, such as the Sun, most astronomers divide them into seven types. Stars fit into each type depending on how hot they are. Usually, the hotter the star, the bigger it is.

O

33,000K or more
(Equivalent to 32,700°C, or 59,000°F.)

Example star in this type: Zeta Ophiuchi

Wait, what does "33,000K" mean?

"K" is short for Kelvin. It's how scientists measure temperatures – especially REALLY hot and cold temperatures.

B

10,500–30,000K
Rigel

A

7,500–10,000K
Altair

F

6,000–7,200K
Procyon

G

5,500–6,000K
The Sun

K

4,000–5,250K
Epsilon Indi

 ## M

2,600–3,850K
Proxima Centauri

What's the brightest star?

It depends on what you mean by _bright_. Astronomers use the word **brightness** to mean the amount of a star's light we can see from Earth. The word **luminosity** describes the total amount of light a star emits.

So what _IS_ the brightest star?

And what's the most LUMINOUS star?

The brightest star is the **SUN**! The _most luminous_ star astronomers have found so far is known as **R136a1**. It's 6 million times more luminous than the Sun.

If you leave a camera pointing at the sky all night long, it won't capture dots of light. Instead, it shows streaks of light called star trails. The trails appear because each star seems to move around the sky.

In fact, we're the ones who are moving. That's because the Earth is spinning around.

What is a constellation?

A collection of stars that, seen from Earth, appears to form a shape. In ancient days, people looked up into the night sky and imagined them as outlines of people, creatures and objects, often from stories.

Here's one...
...Orion the hunter

One way to find constellations is to look for smaller groups of stars known as **asterisms**.

The three stars across the middle are known as Orion's belt: this is an asterism.

Constellations are recognized the world over, while asterisms vary from place to place and are unofficial.

Orion's belt is also:

Frigg's distaff...

(...said the Vikings.)

No, it's the Three Brother star...

(...say people in Malaysia.)

We call it the Bison's spine...

(...say Lakota Native Americans.)

Do constellations have different names?

Yes and no. Over the centuries, different peoples identified their own star patterns, with different names, rarely using the same groups of stars.

Then, in 1930, a group of professional astronomers called the **International Astronomical Union** created an official list of constellations, ensuring that no star was in more than one.

Is there a link between the stars IN a constellation?

None at all. The stars in any part of a constellation are not necessarily close to each other, or joined up. If you looked at them from another planet in the solar system, they'd make similar patterns – but viewed from any other planetary system they wouldn't.

What's the zodiac?

It's a set of twelve constellations. Each constellation is hidden by the Sun at a different point in Earth's year-long orbit. They become visible at roughly the same time each year. From the northern hemisphere, these constellations appear low in the sky. From the southern hemisphere, they appear high up.

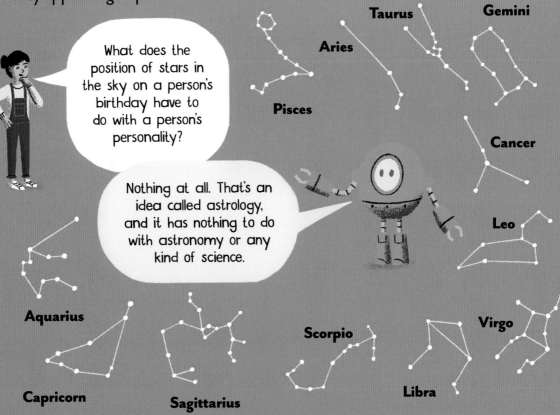

What does the position of stars in the sky on a person's birthday have to do with a person's personality?

Nothing at all. That's an idea called astrology, and it has nothing to do with astronomy or any kind of science.

Taurus

Gemini

Aries

Pisces

Cancer

Leo

Aquarius

Virgo

Scorpio

Capricorn

Sagittarius

Libra

Why do constellations matter?

People across the world and throughout history have used constellations to navigate at night, and to tell stories about their place in the world. And it's fun to spot them!

There are 88 constellations, according to the International Astronomical Union. Every star visible from Earth with the naked eye belongs to just *one* of these 88 constellations.

Lyra

Cygnus

Delphinus

Official name - *What it means*

Andromeda - princess from Greek mythology

Antlia - air pump

Apus - bird of paradise

Aquarius - person carrying water

Aquila - eagle

Ara - altar

Aries - ram

Auriga - charioteer

Bootes - herdsman

Caelum - tool for engraving

Camelopardalis - giraffe

Cancer - crab

Canes Venatici - hunting dogs

Canis Major - big dog

Canis Minor - little dog

Capricornus - sea goat

Carina - the keel of the *Argo*, a legendary Greek ship

Cassiopeia - mother of *Andromeda*

Centaurus - centaur

Cepheus - father of *Andromeda*

Cetus - sea monster

Chamaeleon - chameleon

Circinus - pair of compasses

Columba - dove

Coma Berenices - the hair of legendary Queen Berenice

Corona Australis - southern crown

Corona Borealis - northern crown

Corvus - crow

Crater - cup

Crux - cross

Cygnus - swan

Delphinus - porpoise

Dorado - swordfish

Where do the names come from?

Many are from Greek myths, or are Latin names for animals and tools. Most were named by navigators long, long ago.

Corvus

Crater

Hydra

Draco - dragon

Equuleus - little horse

Eridanus - mythical river

Fornax - furnace

Gemini - twins

Grus - crane

Hercules - mythical Greek hero and demigod

Horologium - clock

Hydra - sea serpent

Hydrus - water snake

Indus - 'The Indian'

Lacerta - lizard

Leo - lion

Leo Minor - little lion

Lepus - hare

Libra - balancing scales

Lupus - wolf

Lynx - lynx

Lyra - lyre or harp

Mensa - Table Mountain

Microscopium - microscope

Monoceros - unicorn

Musca - fly

Norma - carpenter's level

Octans - octant (a navigation tool)

Ophiuchus - person grasping a snake

Orion - mythical hunter

Pavo - peacock

Pegasus - mythical winged horse

Perseus - mythical Greek hero who saved *Andromeda*

Phoenix - phoenix

Pictor - artist's easel

Pisces - fishes

Piscis Austrinus - southern fish

Puppis - stern of the *Argo*

Pyxis - compass on the *Argo*

Reticulum - net

Sagitta - arrow

Sagittarius - archer

Scorpius - scorpion

Sculptor - sculptor's tools

Scutum - shield

Serpens - serpent

Sextans - sextant (a navigation tool)

Taurus - bull

Telescopium - telescope

Triangulum - triangle

Triangulum Australe - southern triangle

Tucana - toucan

Ursa Major - big bear

Ursa Minor - little bear

Vela - sail of the *Argo*

Virgo - young woman

Volans - flying fish

Vulpecula - fox

Scorpius

Libra

How are stars created?

From the dust, gas and debris left behind when old stars (and their surrounding planets) explode. Here's how it happens.

In the VAST gap in between stars, known as the **interstellar medium**, there are places where gigantic clouds of dust and gases, known as **nebulae**, swirl and mingle.

Every single particle in those clouds has a small amount of gravity – the force that pulls objects towards each other.

Over time, gravity helps build up those separate particles into clumps.

How long does this take?

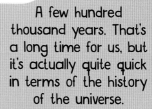

A few hundred thousand years. That's a long time for us, but it's actually quite quick in terms of the history of the universe.

As these clumps grow bigger, they join with other bits, and get bigger and BIGGER and more powerful.

Eventually, two things begin to happen:

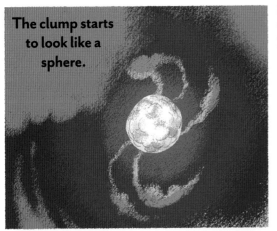

The clump starts to look like a sphere.

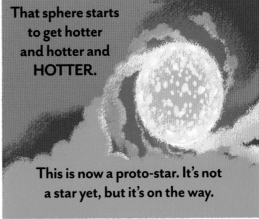

That sphere starts to get hotter and hotter and HOTTER.

This is now a proto-star. It's not a star yet, but it's on the way.

Any objects in the space close to the proto-star get pulled into it, making it bigger, denser and hotter.

Meanwhile tiny pieces of dust and gas start to form into a long, flat disc around the proto-star.

Eventually, the long flat disc forms into planets, asteroids and comets...

...and after a million years or so, the proto-star has now become a MAIN SEQUENCE STAR – just like the Sun.

Do stars ever stop shining?

Yes – stars don't shine forever. They all stop being stars, one way or another. What keeps stars going is the amount of stuff in them that can fuse. But, eventually, that stuff forms into pieces that are too big to keep on fusing.

How long do stars live?

A few billion years – at least, if we're talking about Main Sequence stars, such as the Sun. But there are some types of stars that don't live long at all...

... REALLY MASSIVE STARS. Stars that are MILLIONS of times bigger than the Sun.

> What happens to those kinds of stars?

> After a few hundred thousand years of fusing... they explode!
>
> The outer layers of stuff fly away at fantastic speeds, accompanied by a burst of light called a SUPERNOVA.

Meanwhile, the cores of these stars contract and contract and *contract* – until all that's left is a small but powerful **neutron star**...

...or an incredibly powerful **black hole**.

47

What's a galaxy?

A mind-bogglingly vast collection of stars. But most of the galaxies we can see from Earth are so far away they often look as if they're just points of light. When you look through a powerful telescope, though, you can see that galaxies come in various shapes. Here are a few.

What type of galaxy is that? How big is it?

It's called a SPIRAL GALAXY, because its stars form a spiral shape. This one is hundreds of thousands of light years wide.

Barred spiral – this one has two spirals, joined by a central bar.

Irregular – some galaxies are made up of stars that don't form ANY clear shape.

Elliptical – some galaxies DO have a clear shape, often a squashed circle or **ellipse**.

How many galaxies are there?

At least one TRILLION. But some astronomers think there could be twice as many as that. Using space telescopes, people have been able to see galaxies so far off that their light has taken 13 billion years to reach Earth...

This image was captured by the Hubble Space Telescope. It shows something called the eXtreme Deep Field – a small location in space, containing over 10,000 galaxies.

Yuri Gagarin

Neil Armstrong

I was the FIRST.

I made it to the Moon.

CHAPTER 4

People in space

Who has been to space?

More than 550 people have been to space.
Some have just had a short flight into the upper
atmosphere, while a handful have flown all
the way to the Moon.

Others have spent many months up in the
International Space Station – sometimes
more than once.

I might not be a person...
but I've been to space too!

Ham

Is everyone who goes to space an astronaut?

Kind of! In different places, they have different names. People from America and Europe who go to space are called *astronauts*. From Russia, they're called *cosmonauts*, and from China, *taikonauts*.

> Are astronauts and cosmonauts different?

> They're the same job, they just have different names. Astronaut means *star sailor*. Cosmonaut means *universe sailor*.

Can you explore space without going into space?

Absolutely. People have only been going to space for the last 60 years. But they've been fascinated by the universe for *thousands* of years.

Since ancient times, people have identified planets and stars and watched their journeys through the night sky. They've used those journeys to tell time, mark days and find their way around at night. This is all a kind of science known as **astronomy**.

> Follow that star above the horizon. It will take us southwest.

How did people explore space before rockets?

With all sorts of gadgets – from sticks to super-telescopes.
Here are some of the things people have used to explore space over the centuries.

Over 2,000 YEARS AGO
Maya civilization, Mexico

FORKED STICKS like this one help us to observe the path of Venus.

We've used our observations to create a calendar.

Across Europe 400 YEARS AGO

This is one of the first TELESCOPES. This Italian genius, Galileo, built it himself!

In Persia 1,200 YEARS AGO

This is an ASTROLABE – a small metal disc with over 1,000 different functions...

...from identifying planets to calculating the time.

What did Galileo see?

He saw four moons moving around Jupiter, the first time anyone had seen moons around another planet.

What's inside a telescope?

The main parts are mirrors.
The mirrors collect and concentrate light onto an eyepiece. You can see what the telescope sees by looking into that eyepiece.

Early telescopes used curved pieces of glass called lenses, but mirrors are lighter and easier to use.

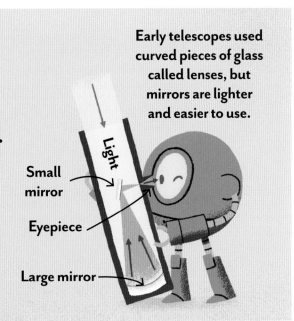

Light

Small mirror

Eyepiece

Large mirror

In the USA, in **1956**

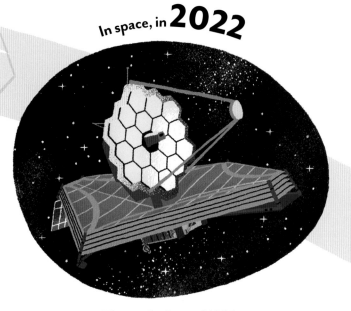

CRACKLE

Wow!

This is a different type of telescope – a RADIO telescope, which picks up radio waves from the sky and space. In 1969, one was used to receive signals from astronauts on the Moon.

In space, in **2022**

This is the James Webb Telescope, which was launched into space by a rocket in 2021. It uses an enormous mirror to take photos of distant galaxies.

When did people first go to space?

In 1961, Yuri Gagarin became the first person in space. From the 1950s, people started sending objects up into space, and exploration changed dramatically. Teams of scientists in different nations were *racing* to be the best at getting things up there, from satellites to people. This period became known as the **space race**.

The two major players in the race were political enemies and bitter rivals:

THE USA

vs

THE USSR

The USSR, also known as the Soviet Union, existed from 1922 to 1991 and was based around Russia.

On your marks... set...

...GO!

OCTOBER 1957
Sputnik 1 becomes the first satellite in space.

APRIL 1961
Yuri Gagarin is the first person in space.

MAY 1961
Alan Shepard is the first American in space.

So who won the space race?

Everybody won! Thanks to the efforts of both the Soviet and American teams, many space milestones were reached.

Why was it a competition?

Each nation wanted to prove it was more powerful than the other. Today Russian and American space agencies work together to explore further – it's not a race any more.

FINISH LINE

JUNE 1963
Valentina Tereshkova is the first woman in space.

DECEMBER 1968
Apollo 8 astronauts orbit the Moon.

JULY 1969
Neil Armstrong steps onto the Moon for the first time.

How did people actually get to the Moon?

Using a rocket, a spacecraft and a lander. The spacecraft used were all called Apollo; the first one to get people to the Moon was called Apollo 11. Here's how it all worked.

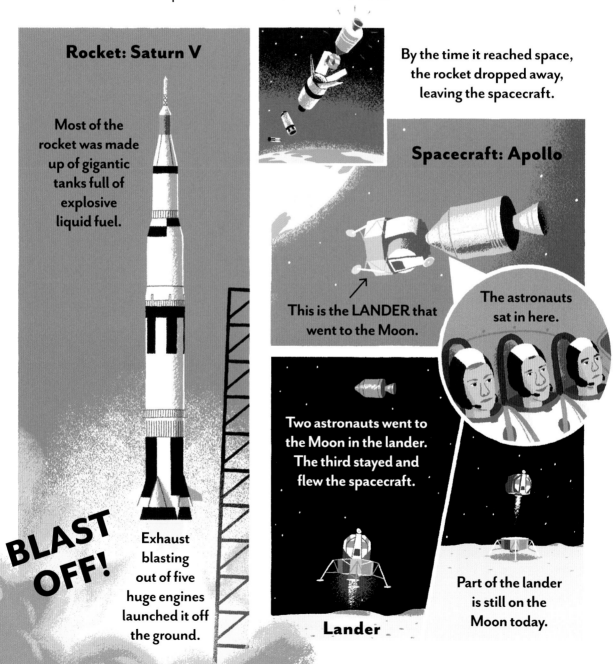

Rocket: Saturn V

Most of the rocket was made up of gigantic tanks full of explosive liquid fuel.

By the time it reached space, the rocket dropped away, leaving the spacecraft.

Spacecraft: Apollo

This is the LANDER that went to the Moon.

The astronauts sat in here.

Two astronauts went to the Moon in the lander. The third stayed and flew the spacecraft.

BLAST OFF!

Exhaust blasting out of five huge engines launched it off the ground.

Lander

Part of the lander is still on the Moon today.

What is being on the Moon like?

So far, only 12 people know the answer to that question.
Everything that the rest of us know is from *their* experiences.
They have tried to describe it in different ways.

"Moon dust is fine, dark and powdery, but razor-sharp. It smells like gunpowder."

"Footprints left on the Moon, even 50 years ago, are still there. There's no wind or weather to blow them away."

"The Moon itself is silent – but there's a constant chatter from the Mission Control people on Earth, as well as the whirring of machinery inside the space suits."

"Walking on the Moon is like walking on a giant trampoline, and the easiest way to move is to bounce along."

Mission Control to Armstrong, can you hear us?

Bzzzz

Whrrr

Hearing you loud and clear!

How dangerous was it?

Very. Being an astronaut has always been, and will continue to be, a dangerous job. At least eight Americans and six Russians died before anyone reached the Moon. There's a small statue on the Moon for these men, called *Fallen Astronaut*.

Who was the first woman in space?

1. Valentina Tereshkova, 1963 (Russian)
2. Svetlana Savitskaya, 1982 (Russian)
3. Sally Ride, 1983 (American)

Why haven't many women been to space?

For a long, long time, space travel – and in fact all of science – was seen as a MAN'S job. By the time Sally Ride went in June 1983, over 120 men had already gone to space.

Is going to space different for men and women?

The short answer is NO. Whoever you are, and wherever you are from, the challenges of going to space are the same. The longer answer is that some things *do* make a practical difference. For example, the first spacesuits were designed for larger, taller men – so some women and smaller men needed different ones.

What's the problem with a spacesuit that's too big?

It's huge!

A spacesuit that doesn't fit won't keep you safe in space. You need to be able to move and work in it safely.

Where are astronauts from?

By the end of 2021, people from 39 different countries had been to space. Right now the BIGGEST space programs are in the USA, Russia, Europe, China and Japan.

Afghanistan	France	Mexico	Spain
Australia	Germany	Mongolia	Sweden
Austria	Hungary	Netherlands	Switzerland
Belgium	India	Poland	Syria
Brazil	Iran	Romania	UK
Bulgaria	Israel	Russia	Ukraine
Canada	Italy	Saudi Arabia	United Arab Emirates
China	Japan	Slovakia	USA
Cuba	Kazakhstan	South Africa	Vietnam
Denmark	Malaysia	South Korea	

Whether or not YOU make it to space partly comes down to where you live. For example, to be considered by NASA, the American space agency, you need to be an American citizen.

In 2022, there still hadn't been any astronauts from Africa.

But going *into* space is only a small part of what space agencies do. For example, NASA employs all sorts of people from all over the world, to do other parts of their work.

I create food for astronauts.

I design Mars rover parachutes.

I plot the routes of spacecraft.

What goes on in the International Space Station?

It's basically a science lab in space. Since November 2000 there has always been someone in the International Space Station (ISS for short). They all do science experiments of one kind or another, and send their results back down to Earth.

The ISS travels around the Earth every 90 minutes. It is so huge it had to be built IN space. It's made up of lots of sections called **modules** joined together.

These rectangles are huge solar panels. They turn sunlight into electricity to power the whole station.

Why is the ISS a big deal?

The ISS is the most expensive thing ever built. It is made of tens of thousands of separate pieces, that were built in different countries, by people speaking different languages.

The ISS isn't just an amazing piece of technology. It also shows what can be achieved when skilled people from around the world work together.

Greetings from India.

Greetings from Korea.

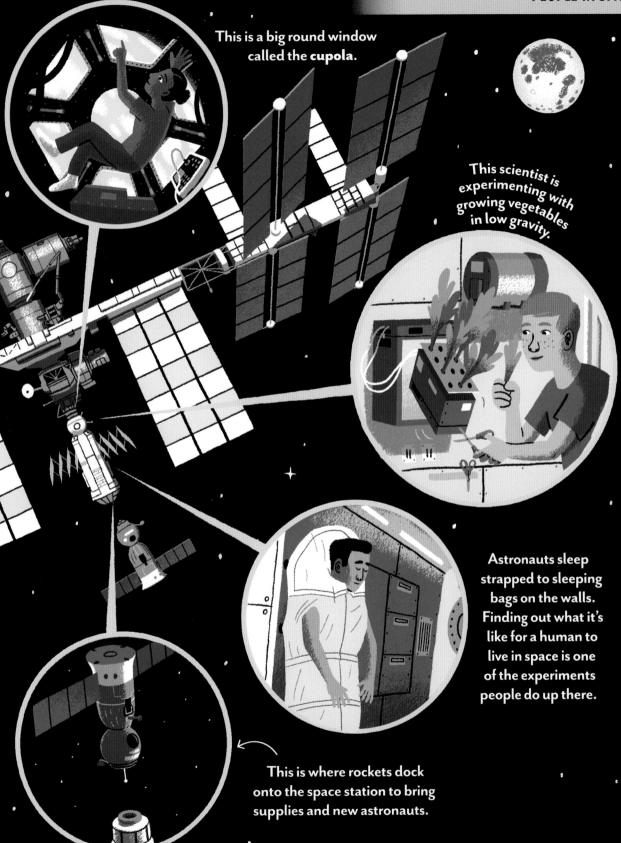

This is a big round window called the **cupola**.

This scientist is experimenting with growing vegetables in low gravity.

Astronauts sleep strapped to sleeping bags on the walls. Finding out what it's like for a human to live in space is one of the experiments people do up there.

This is where rockets dock onto the space station to bring supplies and new astronauts.

61

How do you become an astronaut?

With a lot of training! Here are some of the skills you need to become an astronaut.

Coping under pressure

Staying fit and healthy

Piloting

Hi there.

Privyet.

Konnichi wa.

CORE SKILLS

Engineering

BONUS SKILLS

A university degree in a science subject

Some knowledge of the language and culture of the USA, Russia and Japan

Once you've got those skills and been accepted, the two-year training program begins. Here are some of the things you learn about...

How to cope with STRESS, being hungry, tired and disorientated.

How to SURVIVE in water and in the wilderness.

BONDING with your crew.

What LOW GRAVITY is like.

What to do if communication is difficult, by training underwater.

How to spacewalk, control robotic equipment, and operate the ISS.

Now you are an astronaut!

What happens when you get home?

You see a lot of doctors. The very *first* Moon explorers were kept in secure airtight containers when they got back to Earth, as people worried they may have picked up space-diseases. Today we know that wouldn't be likely, but living up in space *does* have a big impact on your body.

For the first week or two, astronauts can feel extremely **heavy and dizzy.** Adjusting to earthbound life can feel strange...

Some astronauts have noticed **rashes and itchy skin** when they've come home. Earth's air is less clean than the air on a space station.

But why might space life be harmful to our bodies?

Human bodies have evolved to suit the conditions on Earth, not conditions in a space station.

An astronaut's **muscles can waste away** a little. They need to work hard back on Earth to make them stronger again.

Astronauts' bones might change, and get lighter. That can mean their joints get sore or crumbly later in life.

US astronaut Scott Kelly spent a whole year up in space. He has an identical twin brother, who stayed on Earth. Scientists are comparing their bodies as they both get older, to see if all that time in space had a big effect.

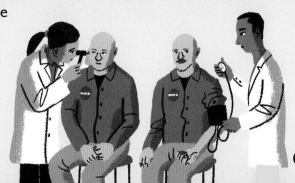

How else have people explored space?

By using machines that can travel further and stay away from Earth longer than humans can. Here are a few of the objects that have been launched to explore our solar system.

Hubble Telescope
Launched 1990

A satellite in orbit around Earth that's also a telescope. It's used to observe and photograph places from across the entire universe.

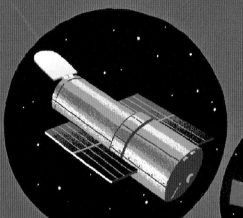

Rosetta Probe
Launched 2004

Landed on a moving comet, 10 years later.

Venera missions
1960s-1980s

A whole series of probes that explored Venus.

Perseverance Rover
Launched 2020

Looking for ancient microbes and signs of LIFE on Mars.

Juno Probe
Launched 2011

Now orbiting Jupiter to find out how it formed, and what it's made of.

Cassini-Huygens mission
Launched 1997

Carried two things to Saturn – the
Huygens Lander, and the Cassini probe.
The probe explored Saturn for 13 years,
taking thousands of amazing photos.

New Horizons probe
Launched 2006

Took photos of Pluto in 2015, having
taken a DECADE to get there.

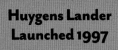

Voyager 2 Probe
Launched 1977

Flew past Uranus and
Neptune, and entered
the outer reaches of the
solar system in 2018.

Huygens Lander
Launched 1997

Landed on Titan,
one of Saturn's
moons, in 2005.
This was the first
human object to
land in the outer
solar system.

Will people ever live on Mars?

Maybe? For now, it's not even possible to visit, let alone live there. But scientists around the world are working on designing spacecraft and equipment to do it. Maybe one day, a long long way into the future, brave astronauts will set up a colony on the planet.

What would a Mars colony look like?

Probably a lot of airtight pods. Mars doesn't have enough oxygen for people to breathe, or enough atmosphere to protect the surface from the Sun's harsh rays. So a colony would have to be COMPLETELY INSIDE.

This is what a colony on Mars COULD look like.

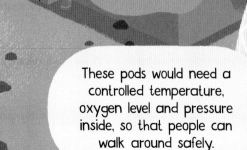

These pods would need a controlled temperature, oxygen level and pressure inside, so that people can walk around safely.

How do we know what Mars is like to live on?

Most of what we know comes from robotic vehicles called ROVERS. Rovers have been exploring Mars for decades.

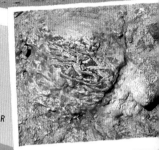

> Rovers have discovered what's in the ground, what the air is like, and taken lots and lots of pictures to send back to Earth.

BEEP
BEEP

INFORMATION
BEAMING BACK
TO EARTH
WHIRRRRRR

What would Martians eat?

Food they've grown themselves. It won't be possible to bring enough food from Earth. Scientists have done experiments in parts of Earth with conditions a little like Mars, and found the best foods to grow there could be...

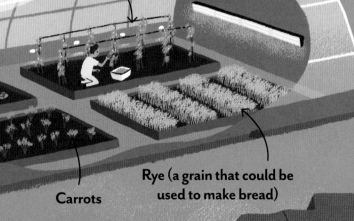

Peas

Lettuce

Carrots

Rye (a grain that could be used to make bread)

CHAPTER 5

The BIGGEST questions

Why do people care about the universe?

Not everybody does... but at some point in their lives, most people look up into space and find themselves asking questions about the universe. WHAT'S out there? WHO'S out there? And what's OUR place in the vast, unknowable universe?

Why did the Big Bang happen?

Nobody knows. People have different theories, but they're very hard to investigate. As far as anyone knows... it just *happened*. Frustratingly, scientists know an awful lot about exactly *what* happened, and in what sequence – within the very first fraction of a second – but not *why* it happened.

> If people knew the answer, would it make us happier?

> Probably not. Finding answers to things often creates a feeling of *satisfaction*, but there's no guarantee it'll make you feel *happy*...

Are people special?

Yes and no. Every individual living thing IS special. That's because the chances of it existing in the first place are very small. But if you compare any one living thing to something the size and timespan of the WHOLE UNIVERSE...

...none of us is special.

> I find it comforting to imagine myself as a small part of the great big whole of everything...

Why is gravity so important?

Because it explains so much about how the universe works.
Gravity is the name for a force that makes objects pull on each other.
People could (and do) spend their entire lives learning about it,
but it can be boiled down to a few key points.

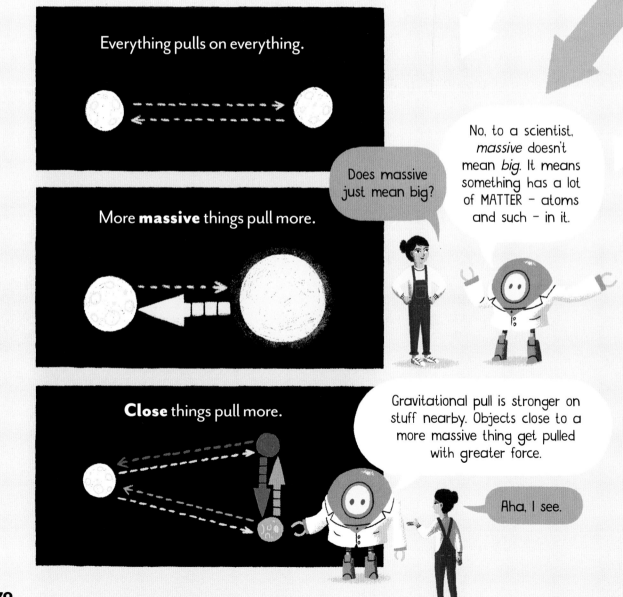

Everything pulls on everything.

More **massive** things pull more.

Does massive just mean big?

No, to a scientist, *massive* doesn't mean *big*. It means something has a lot of MATTER – atoms and such – in it.

Close things pull more.

Gravitational pull is stronger on stuff nearby. Objects close to a more massive thing get pulled with greater force.

Aha, I see.

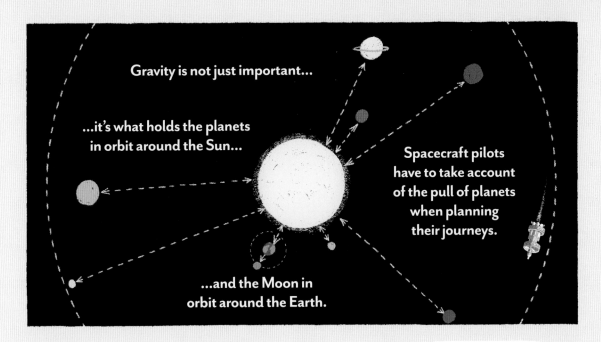

Gravity is not just important...

...it's what holds the planets in orbit around the Sun...

Spacecraft pilots have to take account of the pull of planets when planning their journeys.

...and the Moon in orbit around the Earth.

What does gravity mean for us down on Earth, though?

Earth's gravitational pull is enough to let us stand, but not so strong we are crushed.

Gravity is what helps maintain the Earth's atmosphere.

It also gives us TIDES. Gravity from the Moon pulls water on Earth towards it as it orbits.

OK, I understand all of that. But where does gravity actually come from?

Excellent question! Unfortunately, I can't answer it. For that we need the help of a world-famous physicist and fellow cosmos-ponderer – Albert Einstein.

Hello!

What did Einstein say?

Well, even Einstein would admit no one fully understands the origins and workings of gravity. But what he did say was that things aren't pulling each other closer together – they're actually making space itself *bend*. Here's part of his explanation of what gravity does.

Imagine space like a big blanket, stretched out.

Now put a heavy ball on that blanket, and imagine it's the Sun. The ball is so heavy that the blanket bends around it.

Now let's add another ball, to represent the Earth. The curve around the Sun means Earth *looks as if* it's being pulled towards the Sun.

But gravity is not *really* a pull – it's the effect of big things *bending spacetime*, which makes nearby things move closer.

And do you know what has the most powerful gravity of all? It's a black hole...

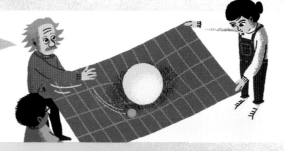

What's a black hole?

It's the remains of a MASSIVE star that has exploded.
Black holes are made of SO MUCH stuff, packed together SO TIGHTLY, that they have an absolutely enormous pull of gravity. They're so strong that any light inside can't escape into space. But black holes are often orbited by swirling dust and gases that do give off light.

The region around a black hole where light stops being able to escape is called the event horizon.

Is that the hole in the middle?

No! It's not a *hole*. It *looks like* a hole because you can't see what's there – but a black hole is actually a physical object.

What would happen if I went into a black hole?

You'd experience some pretty bizarre space and time stretching effects – and you'd never get out of it again.

The swirls of dust and gas around a black hole make up something called an accretion disc. If any of it passes beyond the event horizon, it can no longer be seen.

How long does it take to travel through space?

It depends where you're going. But getting to most destinations in space, in a spacecraft of ANY kind, takes a VERY long time.

Don't spaceships travel REALLY FAST?

Well, yes. Some can reach speeds of over 58,000km/h (36,000mph). Which is stupendously fast compared to cars or trains or even planes, but space is ENORMOUS. Even at that speed, it'd take...

...around 8 months to reach Mars

...around 2 years to reach Jupiter

...around 9 years to reach Pluto

...and around 70,000 years to reach the next nearest star system.

Can't we go any faster?

Definitely – but there are lots of practical problems to solve first.
The spacecraft we know how to build already are expensive. Building better, faster ones will cost a lot more money, and take a lot of time and resources, too.

What new kinds of spaceships are there?

How about this one? It uses sails that are pushed by something called the SOLAR WIND.

This capsule is a just a small box...

...and its sails are far bigger than on a yacht.

This craft could, in theory, get up to 108 million km/h (67 million mph).

How does it work?

Light from the Sun isn't made of nothing. It's made of very small parts called photons.

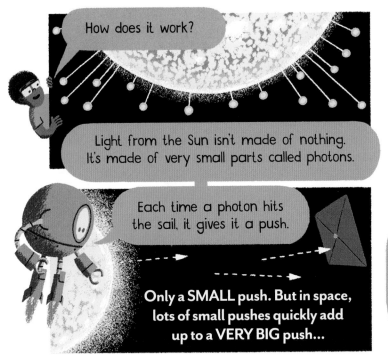

Each time a photon hits the sail, it gives it a push.

Only a SMALL push. But in space, lots of small pushes quickly add up to a VERY BIG push...

Why aren't we using solar sails already?

We are! But only for very small spacecraft. To pull a big one with a human crew, you'd need sails that are many times taller and wider than the ISS. Too big for us to get into space – for now.

What else is out there?

Much more than we can see. Looking out into space, people have seen all sorts of awe-inspiring things, from comets to planets, moons and stars. But there are lots of things we know are out there, that we can't necessarily *see* – things with outlandish names such as **neutron star**, **pulsar** or **magnetar**...

What's a... neutron star?

An incredibly small, but tremendously massive, star. Imagine all the atoms inside the Sun packed together so tightly that they fit inside a ball just 20km (12.5 miles) across. That's what a neutron star is like.

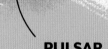

PULSAR

Some types of neutron stars spin around and send out pulses of radiation from their poles. Known as **pulsars**, they're spotted by radio telescopes.

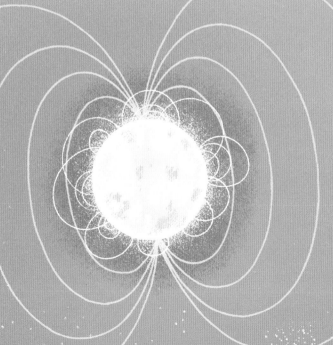

MAGNETAR

There are some neutron stars that no one has EVER seen. Named **magnetars**, they're surrounded by powerful magnetic fields, that send out bursts of all kinds of radiation.

If we found one, we'd be able to see the magnetar itself – but there's no way yet to "see" its magnetic fields.

What's the weirdest object in space?

Most weird objects are only weird because we don't understand what they are... yet.
Here are a few unsolved mysteries of astronomy.

'OUMUAMUA, also known as the "space cucumber," is a long, thin, red rock that is tumbling its way through the solar system, on a journey that began... somewhere UNKNOWN.

HOAG'S OBJECT ...is a ring-shaped galaxy, made up of separate star clusters. How it came to have this shape remains... UNKNOWN.

TABBY'S STAR ...is a bright light in the night sky occasionally obscured by... something UNKNOWN.

Will we ever understand these things?

Using data from new telescopes, one day we probably will.

I want to see something in space that could only exist because aliens built it...

Who else is out there?

As far as we can tell, no one else is out there.
But there MAY be other living things in the universe... somewhere...
Scientists and philosophers agree that there's no reason to think
Earth is SO SPECIAL that it's the *only* place in the universe that
has living and thinking beings on it. But we haven't found
hard evidence of life anywhere else.

Are people looking
for aliens?

Yes. People have
beamed radio
messages into space,
and are listening
out for replies.
So far... they've
heard nothing.

Where are all the aliens?

If there is anyone out there, they will be very, VERY far away.
There's SO MUCH universe, all the livings things in it are likely to
be enormously spread out from each other. Even if they wanted to visit,
we have no idea how long it would take them to reach us.

Shhhh!

And maybe they wouldn't
want to talk to us anyway...

What will aliens look like?

They MIGHT look a lot like us. Or they might look *unimaginably* different.
The only kinds of living things we know about are the ones that live on Earth. If aliens live on a planet that's even a *little* bit like Earth, there's good reason to think they might have features we could recognize.

What sort of features?

Eyes, limbs, tentacles, antennae... that sort of thing.

What counts as an alien?

An alien is any living thing that comes from somewhere that isn't planet Earth. To be a living thing, it has to be able to EAT, BREATHE and to REPRODUCE. This definition includes super tiny things such as bacteria.

So we might have to check for aliens using a microscope?

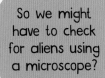

Yes! Also, some scientists think we should look out for robotic rovers and probes. That's how we explore space after all, so aliens might too.

So, the first aliens we meet might actually be robots? Fascinating!

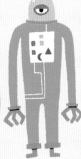

How much does it cost to go to space?

Around $50 million. That's what NASA, the US Space Agency, reckons it spends for each individual astronaut to go to the ISS. For a simple trip to fly above the Kármán Line and back, some companies claim they'd charge $250,000 – once they've figured out how to make this safe and easy.

Why does it cost so much?

NASA isn't just paying for a trip. It's also paying for years of training. And not just the astronauts – it takes a TEAM to prepare and run each and every space mission.

You have to fill a rocket with fuel each time you use it, and fuel costs more than $2 million per launch.

A new spacecraft has to be built for nearly every journey.

Paying people to do a really difficult job is a big and vital part of the cost.

Is space worth the cost?

You decide. Some people argue that all the money spent on finding out about space could be better spent on Earth – for example, curing diseases, or feeding people. Others argue that flying to the Moon and landing robots on Mars are two of the most impressive things humans have ever achieved.

Human curiosity about space, and the need to solve space-based problems, has given the world wonderful inventions. Here are just a few of them.

Ultra-safe firefighting suits, made from materials designed to protect astronauts from direct sunlight

LED lights

Air and water purifiers

Cameras small enough to fit in a phone

Memory-foam mattresses

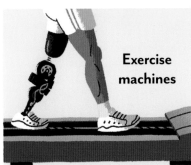

Exercise machines

Sophisticated prosthetics, based on machines used to do space repairs

Instantaneous worldwide communication, thanks to satellite networks

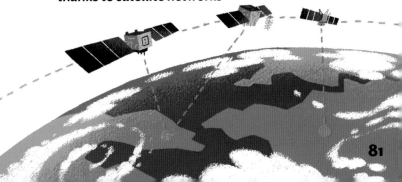

What IS the universe made of?

Sorry, that's not a valid question.
It isn't a "thing" that is "made of" other things. But we CAN talk about the types of things it *contains*, such as atoms, and things made of atoms. But all that atomic stuff that we can see and touch and detect with instruments only makes up...

...about 4% of the Universe.

4%?!! That's nothing. So what does the rest of the universe contain?

We're pretty sure that another 22% is made of something that we can't see called DARK MATTER.

How do we know it's there, then?

Because we can feel its *effects*. Dark matter is what causes a big part of the pull of gravity we feel in the Milky Way.

Here on Earth, those effects have been felt in sophisticated labs, too.

Atomic matter

Dark matter

But there's more. The universe is expanding, but not in a way that makes sense if it's *only* because of dark matter and atomic matter. There seems to be *something else* affecting the universe. But it's a total mystery. Scientists call it... DARK ENERGY.

Dark energy

Why do people study space?

For lots of reasons. But an awful lot of it is about searching for answers to unanswered questions.

BIG questions

What EXACTLY does the universe contain?

What happened before the Big Bang?

What's going on in a black hole?

Serious money

What can I dig up from an asteroid, and how much can I sell it for on Earth?

Can anyone start a big space tourism business?

Major discoveries

Will we ever find life outside of Earth?

Will anyone ever build machines that can transport people beyond our solar system?

Bold new frontiers

Could people ever live, in large numbers, in space stations?

...or on moons?

...or on other planets?

How will the universe end?

In complete silence and total darkness. At least, that's what most scientists say. The universe has been expanding ever since the Big Bang. As far as experts are able to predict, it will simply keep on expanding...

...until every single atom is so far apart from every other atom that there will be NO sound, NO light, and NO way to tell if time is passing any more.

When will this happen?

SO FAR in the future, scientists can't begin to agree on when.

What will happen to us?

We don't know – but we have some idea of what *might* happen.
Planet Earth will be likely to keep going for another few billion years.
During this time, the Sun will gradually expand, and its heat will
gradually boil off the oceans, making the planet uninhabitable.

I wonder what that'll
be like? Is it like
the climate crisis
happening today?

No. The climate crisis
in the 21st century is
harming the planet
plenty – but it's not
boiling off the oceans.

So we don't need to
worry about the world
ending soon, then?

What if we get
hit by a rock
from space?

Well, it's likely that a REALLY BIG space
rock *will* hit the Earth at some point in the
next 50 million years. It's happened before,
and made a lot of animals extinct.

Like the dinosaurs?

Exactly. But next time it
happens, humans might be able
to prevent the worst damage.

Any other questions?

Here are a few of the most commonly asked space questions on the internet...

What things on Earth can you see from Space?

It depends how close you are to Earth, and what you're looking through. From the ISS, you can see mountains, deserts and forests.

Is there weather in space?

Sort of. As well as light, the Sun releases a steady stream of other particles that moves through the solar system at different rates. It's known as **the solar wind**, and it can damage satellites and other space equipment.

Why is Mars red?

There's red dust on much of its surface and in its atmosphere.

Why is space black?

Because there's nothing there for light to bounce off.

What's the Moon made of?

Rock.

Why don't the planets fall into the Sun?

Because they're all moving very fast on a path that would lead them away from the Sun... if the Sun's gravity wasn't pulling them back. This makes them move in elliptical paths around the Sun.

Which space movie has the most accurate physics?

Most activities in space are slow, and journeys are long – and it's tough to make movies that show this properly but keep them fun to watch, too.

These movies depict space travel in a way that breaks very few rules of physics:

2001: A Space Odyssey (1968); Apollo 13 (1995); Gravity (2013); The Martian (2015)

What's left to know?

Lots! Here's a list of some BIG questions that are in need of answers.

How did the universe begin? Is ours the only universe?

If not, is there a way to reach any other one?

How does gravity work, exactly?

Does dark matter really exist, and if so, what is it?

What else does the universe contain, and why can't we see it?

Are there such things as wormholes – and will we be able to find them?

Are the stars we can see still out there?

Are there any places beyond Earth where humans might be able to live?

Can we explain the expanding of the universe – and will it ever stop?

What's it like in a black hole?

Which came first, black holes at the heart of most galaxies, or the galaxies themselves?

Are there aliens anywhere nearby?

Will we ever be able to talk to them?

How can I explore the universe?

In lots of different ways. You don't have to be a grown up, or have any kind of special training. But it's easier if you have access to the internet, or even your own telescope.

Stargaze

Anybody can scan the night sky, with or without a telescope. But it's best to find a really DARK place to do it, away from cities and lights.

Write a story, or draw a picture

Many space scientists were inspired to do their job by reading totally fictional accounts of what space might be like. One of the oldest was Jules Verne's novel *A Voyage to the Moon* in 1856. Science Fiction storytellers still inspire real-life scientists today.

Be an at-home scientist

Observatories around the world share their telescope's views online. You can look at them too, and join researchers – and thousands of amateur astronomers – all hoping to spot new things. Doing stuff like this is sometimes called **citizen science**.

Share your computer

You can ask your computer to use some of its power to review information from radio telescopes around the world. If a computer finds a pattern in those signals, it might just be a sign of communication from another planet.

Be curious

Ask questions

Astronomers love answering people's questions – especially if you can think up a question no one else has asked before. Hunting for an answer might reveal new information about the universe.

Jobs in space

Just as there are lots of ways to explore the universe without leaving the planet, there are all sorts of different jobs that grown-ups do relating to space, from building rockets to researching stars. Here's just a short list of different professions that could take you out into the universe.

An astrobiologist... looks for signs of life beyond Earth, and tries to determine what alien life might be like.

An astronaut... is any trained professional who goes on missions off-planet.

An astronomer... researches what exists in the universe, and how it all works. (They're sometimes known as astrophysicists.)

A chemical engineer... develops the fuels needed to power rockets and spacecraft.

A cosmologist... studies the universe itself, and how it came to be.

A data analyst... examines all kinds of data, from conditions around a spacecraft during launch to samples collected from asteroids.

A flight control operator... helps plan and monitor spacecraft launches and journeys out of and into Earth's atmosphere.

A fundraiser... persuades rich people, wealthy businesses and governments to invest the vast sums of money needed to make space missions possible.

A journalist... reports to the world at large about the detailed operations of space missions and observatories.

Mission control... is the team in charge of each space mission, carefully plotting and monitoring it all from the ground.

A mathematician... is needed to predict the exact movement of planets, moons and asteroids, and to plot courses for spacecraft to find their way to them.

A roboticist... designs and builds robots, rovers and probes that can do all sorts of jobs out in space, or on other planets.

A rocket scientist... designs, tests and builds rockets to help launch spacecraft.

Glossary

Use this page to learn what some technical words about the universe mean. Words in *italics* have their own entries.

asteroids rocks in space that *orbit* a *star*, but not big enough to be called *planets*

atoms tiny *particles* that make up ordinary *matter*

atmosphere a layer of gas surrounding a *planet* and some *moons*

bacteria very small living things that were some of the first life forms on Earth

black holes the remains of some *stars* that have exploded, that have immensely strong gravitational pulls.

Big Bang the event that began all of *spacetime*

comet a ball of ice and dust in space that follows *orbits* a *star* in a long loop described as eccentric.

constellation a collection of *stars* that appears to form a pattern

Cosmic Microwave Background Radiation (CMBR) traces of radiation from the *Big Bang* that can be detected as microwaves

dark matter an unknown type of *matter* that makes up 22% of the *universe*

density how tightly packed together the *atoms* are in an object

dwarf planets objects in space that orbit a *star*, but are smaller and less powerful than *planets*

galaxy a GIGANTIC object in space, spanning thousands of *light years*, that holds many millions of *stars*, *planets* and so on.

gravity the force of two objects pulling on each other; the force that keeps Earth in *orbit* around the *Sun*

light year the distance a beam of light travels in a year; a way to describe really long distances in space

magnetar a highly magnetic collapsed *star*

Main Sequence star a star that is still fusing its hydrogen and helium, and giving off heat and light

Martian someone, or something, from Mars

matter another word for "stuff" – mostly things you can see or touch

meteor a space object entering Earth's *atmosphere*, sometimes called a shooting star

molecule a clump of *atoms* that hold together

moons objects that *orbit* around a *planet* or *dwarf planet* – sometimes called "natural satellites"

Moon the only moon to *orbit* Earth

NASA National Aeronautics and Space Administration, part of the US government that explores and researches space

nebula a vast cloud of dust and gases in space

neutron star an incredibly dense object created from the remains of an earlier massive star

orbit (verb) to travel in a looping path around another, larger object (noun) a fixed path taken by a smaller object as it travels around a larger object

particle a VERY tiny portion of *matter*

photon a tiny, massless *particle* of light

planet an object in space that *orbits* a *star*

plasma a form of any gas where some *particles* can move more freely between *atoms* in the gas. In *stars*, plasma is often extremely hot.

probe a vehicle or machine with no people inside, used to explore a new place

pulsar a spinning *neutron star* that emits a beam of *radiation* from its poles

radiation *particles* and *photons* emitted by objects

red giant a large and relatively cool *star*

rocket a device, full of fuel, that pushes a *spacecraft* so hard that it can escape Earth's gravitational pull

rover a device that drives across *planets* and *dwarf planets,* exploring the terrain and collecting valuable information

satellite a machine in *orbit* that sends and receives signals from its host *planet*

solar panel a device that captures light and converts it into electricity

solar system the part of space in which objects are in *orbit* around the *Sun*

spacecraft a vehicle that can travel through space

spacetime a term to describe the *universe* mathematically, that combines dimensions of space and time

star a huge object in space that continuously fuses its own *atoms* together, creating a long-lasting source of heat and light

Sun the *star* around which Earth and the *solar system* move

supernova an explosion caused by the collapse of a massive *star,* that shines as brightly as a *galaxy* for a few months

universe, the everything that exists in time and space

vacuum the total absence of *matter*

wavelength the name to describe the different shapes of wave that light travels in, including visible light

white dwarf a late stage in a star's life, when it is no longer fusing *atoms,* but still releases *radiation*

wormhole a tunnel linking two distant places (and times) in the *universe.* Wormholes are possible in theory, but scientists don't know for sure that they exist.

Index

Acknowledgements

Who wrote this book?

Alice James and Alex Frith

Who illustrated it?

David J Plant

Who designed it?

Zoe Wray and Tabitha Blore. Stephen Moncrieff designed the cover.

Who checked the facts?

Dr. Ed Bloomer, Royal Observatory Greenwich

Who edited it?

Jane Chisholm

Art Director: Mary Cartwright

Where did the photographs come from?

4-5: Tarantula nebula © NASA/JPL-Caltech. 9: Perseid meteor shower © NASA/Bill Ingalls. 13: Crab nebula © NASA, ESA, G.Dubner IAFE, CONICET-University of Buenos Aires et al; A. Loll et al; T. Temim et al; F. Seward et al; VLA/NRAO/AUI/NSF; Chandra/CXC; Sitzer/SPL-Caltech; XMM-Newton/ESA; and Hubble/STScl. 25: Hale Bopp © Detlev Van Ravensswaay/Science Photo Library (SPL). 28: Earth © NASA Goddard. 30: Venus © NASA/JPL-Caltech. 31: Mars © NASA/JPL/Malin Space Science Systems. 36: Sun © NASA Goddard. 39: Star trails ©Amirreza Kamkar/SPL. 40: Orion © ESA/Hubble/Akira Fujii. 48: Spiral galaxy © NASA Goddard. 49 eXtreme Deep Field © NASA Goddard. 57: Footprint © NASA, Moonwalk © NASA/JSC. 67: Mars surface © NASA/JPL-Caltech/MSSS, Mars rocks © NASA/JPL-Cltech/LANL/CNES/IRAP/LPGNantes/CNRS/IAS/MSSS. 86-87: Small Magellanic Cloud © NASA/CXC/JPL-Caltech/STScl.

First published in 2022 by Usborne Publishing Ltd., Usborne House, 83-85 Saffron Hill, London, EC1N 8RT, United Kingdom, usborne.com Copyright © 2022 Usborne Publishing Ltd. The name Usborne and the Balloon logo are trade marks of Usborne Publishing Ltd. All rights reserved. No part of this publication may be reproduced, stored in any retrieval system, or transmitted in any form or by any means, without the prior permission of the publisher. Printed in China. First published in the USA in 2022. UE.